I WONDER Why

Planes Have Wings

and other questions
about transportation

Christopher Maynard

KINGFISHER

Published 2012 by Kingfisher
an imprint of Macmillan Children's Books
20 New Wharf Road, London N1 9RR
Associated companies throughout the world
www.panmacmillan.com

First published 1993 by Kingfisher

Consultant: Ian Graham

ISBN 978-0-7534-4064-3

9 8 7

7TR/1218/WKT/UG/115MA

A CIP catalogue record for this book is available from
the British Library.

Printed in China

Illustrations: Mark Bergin cover, 5 (train, car and bike), 8,
11t, 16, 20–1, 30–1 (aircraft); Chris Forsey 4, 5 (plane), 6–7,
17–19, 26 (wagon train), 28–9; Tony Kenyon (B.L. Kearley
Ltd) all cartoons; Sebastian Quigley (Linden Artists) 10, 11b;
Ian Thompson 9, 12–13; Ross Watton (Garden Studio) 14–15,
22–5, 30 (transporter), 31 (ships).

CONTENTS

How far can I go in an hour?

If you keep walking for an hour, and don't stop to take any rests, your own two legs will carry you about 4 kilometres. You will be able to go further if you run, but you will probably have to keep stopping to get your breath back. The easiest way to travel more than a few kilometres is to get something to carry you!

It would take an ordinary garden snail more than three days to get as far as you can walk in one hour.

To walk as far as a jumbo jet can carry you in an hour, you would have to keep going for ten days and nights!

Trotting on a pony for an hour, you would be able to travel three times as far as you would on foot.

Racing cyclists can pedal at least ten times as fast as you can walk. They can cover as much as 40 kilometres in an hour.

Aircraft are the fastest way to travel. Flying high above the clouds in a jumbo jet, you would be able to get from Paris to London in less than an hour.

Riding in a high-speed train like the Japanese Bullet train or the French TGV, you can travel at least twice as fast as you can in a car.

Engines are more powerful than muscles, so machines can carry you much faster than legs. Riding in a car on a motorway, you can travel at more than 100 kilometres an hour!

Even if you stay in bed all day, you will travel about 2.5 million kilometres! That's how far the Earth moves through space in 24 hours, as it goes around the Sun.

Which is the fastest car?

A British car called *Thrust 2* set the world land speed record in 1983. A new record was then set in 1997 by *Thrust SSC*, which reached a speed of 1,228 kilometres an hour.

The first car to go faster than 100 kilometres per hour was battery-powered. It was called *La Jamais Contente*, and it did this over 100 years ago, in 1899.

The world's fastest sailing craft are sailboards. In good winds, they can zip across the water at more than 80 kilometres per hour.

Which is the fastest boat?

Hydroplanes skim over the water almost as if flying. In 1978, Ken Warby roared to 511 kilometres per hour in his jet-powered *Spirit of Australia*.

Spirit of Australia

Thrust 2

To carry astronauts to the Moon in the 1960s and 1970s, the *Saturn V* rockets had to travel more than 40 times as fast as a jumbo jet. But the top speed of the astronauts' moon buggy was only 13 kilometres an hour!

SR-71A *Blackbird*

One of the quickest ways to travel without an engine is on skis.

Which is the fastest plane?

The fastest aircraft are planes with jet engines. The world record was set back in 1976, when the USA's SR-71A reached an amazing 3,530 kilometres per hour! It was nicknamed *Blackbird*.

Why do planes have wings?

Planes have wings for the same reason that birds do – to help them fly. Plane wings work because of their shape. They are curved more on top than underneath, and this makes air flow faster above them than below. The faster air above the wings sucks them upwards.

Which cars have wings?

Wing

Many racing cars have wings. Unlike plane wings, these are more curved underneath than on top. This means they work in the opposite way to plane wings, sucking down rather than up, helping the tyres to grip the track.

We can't flap our arms fast enough to fly like birds. But this didn't stop people trying to copy birds in the days before planes were invented!

Rotor blades

Hydroplane

A helicopter's long, thin rotor blades are wing-shaped – curved more on top than underneath. As they whirl through the air, this wing shape helps the helicopter to fly.

To see how wings work, blow hard over the top of a piece of thin paper. The paper will rise up!

Submarines have short wings called hydroplanes. These are moved up and down to help subs climb and dive.

Which plane is the biggest?

The biggest passenger plane is the A380 airliner. It carries about 525 passengers. They sit on two decks, one above the other. The biggest plane of all is a giant cargo plane called the An-225. Only one was built. It can carry cargo weighing as much as 25 elephants inside its huge body.

The world's largest passenger planes are nicknamed jumbo jets and superjumbos after an elephant called Jumbo. Jumbo was a star attraction at London Zoo in the 1800s.

Can planes hover in the air?

Most planes have to keep going fast through the air to fly. If they slow down and stop, their wings stop working and they can't fly any more. The F-35B Lightning II (above) and the Harrier (below) can hover in one spot above the ground by blasting jets of air straight downwards to hold them up.

Hummingbirds can hover in the air, too. They beat their tiny wings between eight and 80 times per second. They can also fly backwards and upside down!

Harrier fighter planes have been nicknamed jump jets because they can take off straight up into the air.

11

Do airships run on air?

Modern airships should really be called gas ships, because they use a gas called helium to help them to fly. Helium helps airships to float because it is lighter than air.

The bag of an airship is called an envelope.

Fairground balloons are usually filled with helium gas. To see which is lighter, helium or air, try letting go of a fairground balloon at the same time as a party balloon filled with air.

The first 'air' letter was carried by a balloon.

Burner

Why do hot-air balloons float?

Balloons float because hot air rises, and hot air rises because it is lighter than cold air. The air inside a hot-air balloon is heated by a burner, which works rather like a camping gas stove.

The first-ever balloon passengers were a cock, a duck and a sheep! Their 8-minute flight took place over Paris in 1783.

Why do cars have wheels?

Cars and most other land machines have wheels because they make it easier to move. Things slow down when they rub against the ground. Wheels help because they turn easily, and only a small part of them touches the ground.

Imagine how difficult it would be to move a car if all of it was touching the ground, instead of just its wheels!

The world's longest car has 26 wheels! It even has room for a tiny swimming pool on board!

Snow and ice are much more slippery than soil and rock. That's why skis and ice skates don't need wheels!

Which are the biggest tyres?

The world's biggest tyres are made for huge dumper trucks, to cushion their heavy loads of rock and earth. The tyres are over 4 metres high – that's about four times as tall as you are!

The wheelbarrow was invented in China more than 1,800 years ago. It made it easier to carry heavy loads.

Which boats have wheels?

River boats called paddle steamers are driven along by wheels. The wheels have wide boards called paddles. As the wheels turn, the paddles push against the water, moving the boat along.

Why do cars need petrol?

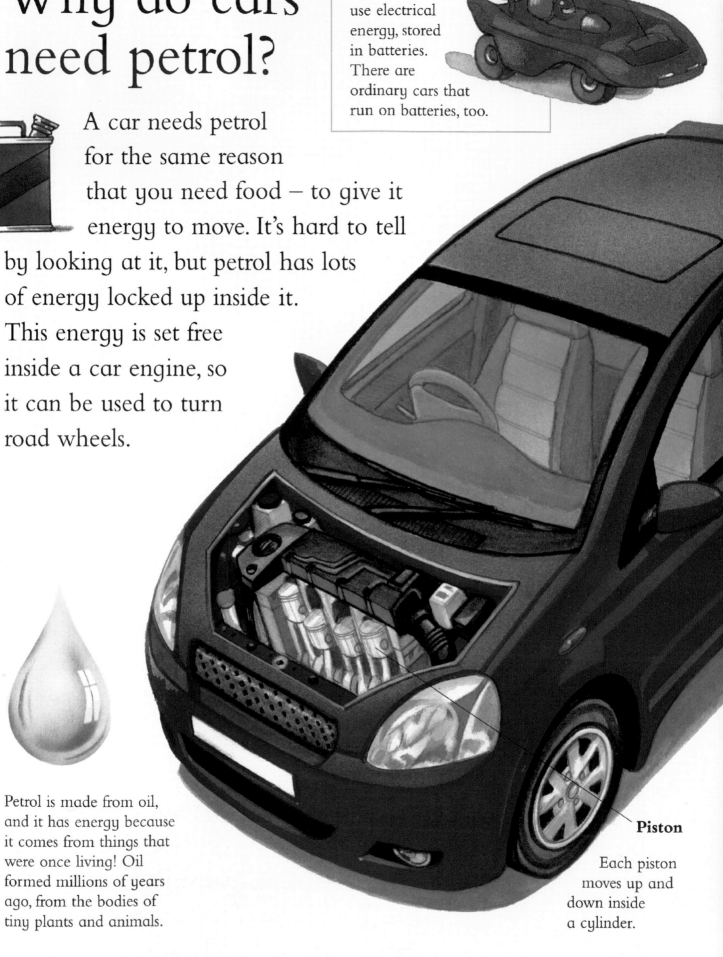

Many toy cars use electrical energy, stored in batteries. There are ordinary cars that run on batteries, too.

A car needs petrol for the same reason that you need food – to give it energy to move. It's hard to tell by looking at it, but petrol has lots of energy locked up inside it. This energy is set free inside a car engine, so it can be used to turn road wheels.

Petrol is made from oil, and it has energy because it comes from things that were once living! Oil formed millions of years ago, from the bodies of tiny plants and animals.

Piston

Each piston moves up and down inside a cylinder.

Petrol is kept in a tank. It is pumped along a pipe to the engine.

Petrol tank

Spark plug

Spark

Piston

Cylinder

Crankshaft

The world's biggest petrol station is in Jeddah, Saudi Arabia. It has over 200 pumps!

What happens inside car engines?

Petrol is mixed with air inside a car engine and then set on fire by an electric spark. This makes the air and petrol explode with a bang. This explosion pushes engine parts called pistons up and down very quickly. The pistons make a rod called the crankshaft spin round. The crankshaft makes other rods spin, and they turn the car's wheels.

Who cycled over the sea?

In June 1979, American Bryan Allen pedalled a special plane called the *Gossamer Albatross* across the Channel, from England to France, in just under 2 hours and 50 minutes. Nine years later, Kanellos Kanellopoulos of Greece pedalled his *Daedalus 88* over the sea between the islands of Crete and Santorini.

Can bikes climb mountains?

Machines called mountain bikes are specially designed for rough, stony ground. Their frames are extra-strong so they can stand up to rattling over bumps, while their knobbly tyres grip well even in slippery sand or mud.

It's not easy to balance on a unicycle – it only has one wheel!

How many people can ride on a bike?

When the first bicycles were invented, about 200 years ago, they didn't have any pedals! People rolled them along by pushing against the ground with their feet.

Although most bikes are designed for one rider, special bikes are sometimes built to take more. A bike was built in Belgium that had seats and pedals for 35 people, but it was very difficult for them all to balance and cycle at once!

Can motorbikes ever fly?

Motorbikes can't really fly because they don't have wings, but stunt riders still do amazing things on them. By speeding up a ramp and taking off from the end, riders can make their machines leap huge distances through the air.

The first motorcycle with a petrol engine was built in 1885. Much of the bike was carved from wood! It was destroyed by fire in 1903.

Which motorbikes have four wheels?

Quad bikes are special cross-country motorbikes with four wheels to grip and balance on rough ground.

Quad bikes are also called All Terrain Vehicles. 'Terrain' means land or ground.

Some motorbikes are called choppers, because they have had bits 'chopped off' and moved around to make them look unusual.

What is the largest human motorcycle pyramid?

For more than two people to ride one motorcycle is difficult and dangerous, but there are stunt riders who do it for special shows. In 2001, the Dare Devils Team of the Indian Army Signal Corps managed to carry 201 people on a line of ten motorcycles at a military parade ground in Jabalpur.

Why don't ships sink?

When things are put into water they make room for themselves by pushing the water aside.

Although ships are heavy, they are hollow with high sides. This means that they can settle quite low in the water, pushing a lot of the water aside. In fact, a ship will not sink unless it is overloaded and becomes heavier than the water it pushes aside.

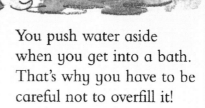

You push water aside when you get into a bath. That's why you have to be careful not to overfill it!

How do submarines sink?

Submarines sink by making themselves too heavy to float. Water is let into special tanks to add weight. When it's time for the submarine to resurface, the water is pushed out.

GOING DOWN

GOING UP

Air out

Air in

Water in

Water out

Which ships fly?

Although hovercraft travel across water, they don't float in it like ships. Instead, they hover just above the waves, held up by a cushion of air.

Hovercraft can travel over land as well as water.

Tanker

One of the earliest submarines was built by Dutchman Cornelius van Drebbel and tested in the 1620s. Twelve oarsmen rowed a wooden boat below the surface of the River Thames, in England.

This strange-looking diving suit was invented over 200 years ago. The tubes carried air to and from the surface.

Which are the biggest ships?

The biggest ships in the world are oil supertankers. They can be over half a kilometre long and weigh more than 1,000 jumbo jets. Giant tankers can take 20 minutes to stop!

Life jackets are only 200 years old. A French priest invented them when he lined a waistcoat with a floaty material called cork.

Some tankers are so long that crews cycle about them!

Tanker

What were longships?

We call Viking ships longships, because of their long, thin shape. The Vikings were people who lived in Scandinavia about 1,000 years ago. They built sturdy wooden ships and were skilful sailors.

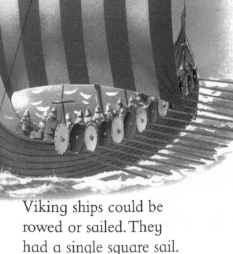

Viking ships could be rowed or sailed. They had a single square sail.

Which are the world's smallest boats?

Coracles are just about the world's smallest boats – they usually only have room for one person!

Sailing boat

Hovercraft

Viking ship

Warships once had small castles on the front and back.

Sterncastle

Forecastle

Ships' hammocks were first used 500 years ago. European sailors copied them from hanging beds they saw in the West Indies.

25

Why don't trains fall off the rails?

Trains have metal wheels and run on narrow metal rails. Metal can be very slippery, so train wheels are specially shaped to stop them falling off. The inside of each wheel has a lip called a flange, which holds it on the rail.

Flange

Rail

Wheel

The wagons rolled along at 1.5 to 3 kilometres an hour.

Some trains can climb steep mountainsides without sliding down. They have an extra wheel with a toothed edge that 'bites' into a notched rail.

Early American locomotives were fitted with plough-like cowcatchers to keep the line ahead clear.

What were wagon trains?

In the 1800s, when settlers spread westwards across North America, they took all their belongings with them in huge wagons drawn by oxen or mules. Families travelled in groups. Their wagons following each other in a long line were called a wagon train.

Do road trains run on rails?

No, road trains run on roads. They are called trains because they are made up of trucks pulling lots of trailers, in the same way that locomotives haul wagons.

Not all trains need drivers. Some city trains are controlled by computers.

Australian trucks and cars often have strong metal bull bars fitted in front, to cut down damage if they hit large animals, such as kangaroos or cattle, on outback roads. Another name for them is roo bars ('roo' is short for kangaroo).

Trams are buses with metal wheels that run on rails. They use electricity to move, taking it from cables stretched high above the road.

Bull bars

Road trains are often used in areas where there are no railway lines – in parts of the Australian Outback, for example.

Can trains float?

Maglevs are a kind of passenger train which float just above a special track. They are lifted and driven by the power of magnets, and they can travel very fast – at over 500 kilometres an hour!

Which plane hitches a ride?

It's not every day that you see one plane hitching a ride on another, but it does happen. A rocket-plane called *SpaceShip Two* is designed to hitch a ride underneath an aircraft called *White Knight 2*. When they reach a height of about 15,200 metres, *White Knight 2* drops *SpaceShip Two*, which fires its rocket engine and soars away into space at 4,000 kilometres an hour.

White Knight 2

SpaceShip Two

Ships can ride piggyback, too, on special heavy-lift ships! First, the heavy-lift ship makes itself sink – not completely, but low enough for a smaller ship to float on to its deck. When it rises up again, the smaller ship gets a ride.

1

2

3

When do cars hitch rides?

It's usually people that hitch rides in cars, but sometimes cars themselves get taken for a ride. It happens when new cars are carried on trucks or trains, from the factories where they are made to showrooms where they are sold.

It may sometimes look as if cars are about to roll off transporters, but don't worry – they are tied firmly in place.

31

Index